RUGBY

Donald Ireland

WORLD OF SPORT

American football

Basketball

Cricket

Cycling

Field athletics

Fishing

Gymnastics

Horse riding

Judo

Rugby

Sailing and windsurfing

Skiing

Soccer

Swimming and diving

Tennis

Track athletics

Editor: Tim Byrne

Cover: The 1987 world cup final between France and the New Zealand All Blacks.

First published in 1988 by
Wayland (Publishers) Ltd
61 Western Road, Hove
East Sussex, BN3 1JD, England

© Copyright 1988
Wayland (Publishers) Ltd

British Library Cataloguing
in Publication Data
    Ireland, Donald, Rugby
    I Rugby football
    I Title   II Series
796.33'3

ISBN 1–85210–159–8

Picture acknowledgements:
All pictures supplied by
ALL SPORT (UK) LTD.
(with thanks to Russell Cheyne)
except page 5(b) BBC Hulton

Designed and typeset by
DP Press Ltd, Sevenoaks, Kent

Printed and bound in Italy
by Sagdos

Contents

History of the game

The game of rugby has spread worldwide to such an extent that the first ever World Cup was held in 1987. Sixteen countries took part and the tournament was such a success that in the future many more countries will participate. Rugby as a major world sport has arrived.

Football of one sort or another has been played since before Roman times. Rules were virtually unknown and the pitch could be up to eight kilometres in length and almost limitless in width. The 'ball' varied between a medium-sized stone to a stuffed pig's bladder. The object of the game was to get the ball across the other side's boundary – no matter how. The game of hurling in Cornwall and la soule in France were both forerunners of the game of rugby but the first game using a pitch as we know it was a Roman game called *Harpastum* (the ancient Greek word for handball).

The ball they used was small, round and hard which

The first World Cup was held in 1987. In this picture, Wade Dooley wins the ball for England, but Australia won the match and went on to the semi-final.

The game of hurling is a forerunner of the modern game of rugby and is still played in Ireland today.

encouraged handling rather than kicking. A score was achieved by depositing the ball over the opposing end line. Was this the forerunner of the try?

With so many variations of the game being played it was difficult for villages or towns to play each other because their rules were so different. It was in fact British schools who first started to regularize the laws of the game. In about 1846 schools divided into two distinct groups – those who allowed handling of the ball and those who didn't.

The school leading the group who played the handling game was Rugby School – hence the name, rugby football.

THIS STONE
COMMEMORATES THE EXPLOIT OF
WILLIAM WEBB ELLIS
WHO WITH A FINE DISREGARD FOR THE RULES OF FOOTBALL
AS PLAYED IN HIS TIME
FIRST TOOK THE BALL IN HIS ARMS AND RAN WITH IT
THUS ORIGINATING THE DISTINCTIVE FEATURE OF
THE RUGBY GAME
A.D. 1823

This plaque commemorates the birth of rugby in 1823 when William Webb Ellis, a pupil at Rugby School, picked up the ball and ran with it. This is how the sport derived its name.

The game of rugby football at Rugby School came into being when in 1823 a pupil named William Webb Ellis picked up the ball and ran, so originating the distinctive feature of the rugby game. Interestingly enough it was not until 1841 that Rugby School itself recognized the picking up of the ball and running with it. By 1880 nearly three-quarters of all club players in England were former pupils of Rugby School and this school's contribution to the game was very significant and important.

At club level, uniformity was achieved with the formation of the Rugby Football Union (RFU) in 1871, when twenty clubs agreed to a drafting of the code of laws. The first international played was in 1871 when Scotland beat England at Raeburn Place, Edinburgh.

In 1905 the first international involving an overseas country was played in London when New Zealand beat England by five tries to nil. The game rapidly spread overseas and in 1888 the first British Isles team toured Australia and New Zealand. In the same year the New Zealand Maoris toured the British Isles.

Many variations of rugby are played throughout the world today in the following ways:

Rugby League

Rugby players do not receive salaries for playing the game, all they can claim are travelling expenses. In the North of England, in the early days of rugby, many club players were miners or mill workers and to play for their club they had to miss work and this cost them money.

The northern clubs wanted to make up their wages but there was much opposition from the rugby union headquarters. In 1895 there was a motion put forward that 'Players be allowed compensation for bona fide loss of time'. The motion was passed and in 1895, twenty-two clubs formed the Northern Rugby Football Union. At first there was a maximum of six shillings a day allowable to be paid in respect of loss of earnings.

One problem the Northern Union had was that if players were to be paid then spectators would have to be attracted to cover this cost. To achieve this the game would have to be faster with far more open play. This meant radical alterations to the laws including: no direct kicking into touch, no line-

(Opposite) Rugby league is very different to rugby union. There are no rucks or mauls, leading to a faster moving game.

outs, no rucks or mauls and, after a tackle, the ball was tapped back by the tackled player. This meant scrums were greatly reduced and there were few rucks and mauls. By reducing the side to thirteen players there was only a passing resemblance to the earlier version of the game and in 1922 the name of the 'Northern Union' was changed to that of 'Rugby League'.

The main element of the new game was competition between clubs. The League Competition, Challenge Cup and Lancashire and Yorkshire Cups provided that competition. The only time rugby union and rugby league players officially got together was during the Second World War when league players were allowed to participate in union games including internationals.

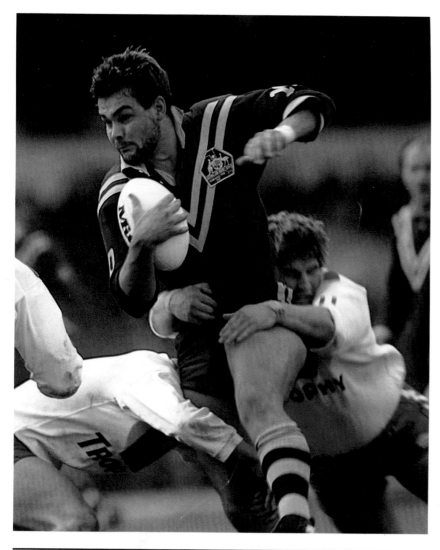

Rugby league is played at international level. In a test match, Paul Dunn (Australia) tries to get through the Great Britain defence.

Although primarily associated with professionalism the game is so popular that there is a flourishing amateur league. Internationals now take place between England, Wales, France, New Zealand and Australia and the number of internationals is likely to increase.

American football

American football is a mixture of rugby and soccer. It developed into a very violent game and there were many injuries some of which were fatal. In 1880 to combat this growing violence, the scrummage was introduced and this helped the game to become more popular. Each team has eleven players on the field and scoring varies from a touchdown (worth six points), field goal (three points), safety (two points) and a try (one point). One of the main differences from any other type of football is that obstruction is allowed. This is known as blocking. In American football today the top stars can earn large amounts of money.

The fast action game of American football has evolved from both rugby and soccer.

Australian rules football

Australian rules football was developed in the late nineteenth century. It is a combination of Gaelic football from Ireland and rugby football. Teams consist of twenty players and the score for a goal is six points and for a behind, one point. There is no try or touch down and all the points come from kicking. The Australian game is unique in that the playing area is oval in shape.

Canadian football

Canadian football is very similar to the American game but the teams have one extra player and you cannot interfere with a running player. Like Australian and Gaelic football international matches are unknown as no other country play these codes of football.

Australian rules football is yet another variation of the game of rugby in another part of the world.

Gaelic football

Gaelic football is distinctly Irish and is reputed to be the roughest of all football games. The accent in this game is on kicking and catching rather than running and passing. If a player wants to make progress down the field he must bounce the ball on his run.

There are fifteen players a side and the ball is round. The posts are similar to rugby ones but there is a net, soccer style, covering the area below the crossbar. If the ball is kicked under the crossbar it is worth three points; above the crossbar it is worth one point. The game consists of two halves of thirty minutes each.

Gaelic football is almost a direct combination of rugby and soccer. Players can pick up the round ball and run with it.

Recent developments

Sponsorship

Up to the 1960s Rugby Union was a game of amateur status and found itself short of the necessary finance to ensure that it expanded. In the early 1970s the RFU accepted that the game would benefit financially from sponsorship and their amateur status would not be affected. This decision meant that the country's administrators were able to use the money to restructure the game. National products in all countries were only too keen to sponsor rugby, from Toshiba in Japan to British Gas in Britain. This interest has been reflected in the success of sponsored league championships and cup competitions throughout the world.

The modern game of rugby relies upon sponsorship for financial survival. Players wear the names of their teams' sponsor on their vests and advertising billboards display the names of championship sponsors.

The World Cup

The inaugural World Cup took place in 1987 in Australia and New Zealand. Although rugby had featured in the Olympic Games up to 1924 – the last winners were the USA – no organized competition on a worldwide basis had taken place since then. With sixteen competing countries, the tournament proved a great success and is now likely to be played on a regular basis every four years. As many as a hundred countries play rugby so it may not be long before there will have to be a series of qualifying matches to decide who will make up the last sixteen. The New Zealand All-Blacks won the 1987 championship.

Seven-a-Side rugby

This fast and exciting variation of rugby started in Scotland in 1882, when a tournament was held at Melrose for all the

The fastest version of rugby is seven-a-side rugby. Using only three forwards and four backs, it is an action packed and thrilling game.

Border clubs. Since then seven-a-side festivals have very much become a feature of the rugby calendar throughout the world. The Hong Kong Sevens is the most prestigious tournament and besides the major rugby playing countries such diverse teams as Bahrain, Netherlands and Thailand competed in the 1987 tournament. Sevens gains in popularity every year as it is a fast, skilful handling game using three forwards and four backs. Because of the speed of the game the duration of matches is limited to fourteen minutes and the final to twenty minutes. The largest tournament is in England when around 300 clubs compete for the Middlesex Sevens.

Mini rugby uses nine players per side and was devised to encourage younger players to enjoy rugby.

Mini rugby

This is a variation of the full game devised in the early 1970s to give young children an enjoyable and instructive start to rugby. So often in fifteen-a-side rugby, certain players –

especially wing three-quarters – may go through a game touching the ball only once or twice. This does not encourage young players to obtain an appetite for rugby. The Welsh Rugby Union set up a committee under Ray Williams their coaching organizer, to find an answer to this problem; and the result was mini-rugby.

The teams are nine-a-side (four forwards and five backs) and the pitch is much smaller. Often the game is played across a normal pitch between the goal line and the twenty-two (see page 33 for the layout of a pitch). Goal posts are not essential as conversions can be taken, using the posts already on the pitch. All conversions are taken in front of the posts twenty metres back. All players have many opportunities to handle the ball while at the same time adhering to the laws of the real game.

Women's rugby

The popularity of this branch of rugby has increased beyond recognition over the past few years. In the British Isles,

Women's rugby is played extensively throughout the world to such high standards that international matches, like this one between France and England, are held.

England and Wales have set up structured leagues and in 1987 the final of the English League Championship was played at Twickenham as a curtain raiser before the men's County Championship final. France runs a highly competitive league and they are perhaps the strongest country in Europe. Italy has come well to the forefront in recent years and Spain and Holland are also making great strides.

Women's rugby is spreading in Africa, and New Zealand now has nearly thirty women's clubs. If New Zealand are the team to beat in men's rugby, their female equivalent would either be the USA or Canada. An immensely popular sport in both these countries, it should not be long before sponsorship is found to promote overseas tours to help resolve which is the best country.

Young fans follow rugby with great enthusiasm. Findlay Calder (Scotland) enjoys the support of his fans.

World game

Europe

England

England have been playing competitive international rugby since 1871 and in the Five Nation Championship since 1910. The backbone of the game in England is club rugby with 2100 clubs playing every weekend. Within this framework are famous traditional fixtures and competitions – the University Match, Hospitals Cup, County Championships, Universities Athletics Union Championship that all contribute to the players getting the opportunity to participate in competitive rugby at a higher level.

In 1972 the Rugby Union introduced the John Player Cup, a knock-out competition. In the 1987/1988 season the Courage League Championships were introduced. 1128 clubs participate in 106 Leagues. As a result, crowd attendance has dramatically increased. In the 1987 World Cup the England team came a close second in the first round play-off, to the Australians.

The 1988 England team.

France

Rugby is especially popular in the south and south-west of France. The game arrived in France in the early 1870s and was centred around Paris. The first club in France was Le Havre and the French Club Championship started in 1892. To many Frenchmen this is the most important rugby tournament and its popularity is such that the final is played in Paris. French rugby is famous for its stylish and attacking play.

Ireland

In Ireland rugby is one sport where both the Republic of Ireland and Northern Ireland combine to portray a united front. The game spread throughout Ireland via the colleges and universities. The first club formed was Trinity College, Dublin and the first town club was the North of Ireland Football Club in Belfast. League and Cup Competitions

The 1988 French team. French rugby is famous for its stylish and attacking play.

have been prominent since 1882 when the Irish Senior Cup was first contested. Home international matches are now played in Dublin but until 1954 Belfast was also a regular venue for internationals.

Italy

Rugby 'arrived' in Italy in 1911 but it was not until 1936 that the first international was played, against France. Italian Club rugby is dominated by the Club League Championship which like many other European countries is played on Sunday rather than Saturday. There is now a national structure and teams at Under-19 and Under-15 level have played international matches.

Romania

Rugby didn't reach Romania until 1912/13 but within eleven years they competed in the 1924 Olympic Games. Romania owes much to France because the students at French universities helped to spread the game and the French were Romania's first international opponents. Although Romania has beaten France, Wales and Scotland they have had difficulties in organizing international fixtures on a regular basis.

The 1988 Ireland team. In Ireland rugby has been played for over one hundred years.

Scotland

Since taking part in the first ever international match against England in 1871, Scotland has been one of the world's leading rugby countries. The game grew in Scotland through the schools and universities. For over fourteen years Scotland has had a league system for their clubs and these now total some 120. At international level, the annual match played against England for the Calcutta Cup attracts the greatest interest among both players and spectators.

The 1988 Scottish side. Scotland is one of the world's leading rugby-playing countries.

Wales

Although Wales is one of the smallest rugby countries, it has one of the greatest reputations in the world of rugby. The game is concentrated in the south around the coal mining areas and such is the love of the game that even the smallest villages can produce a team. This has resulted in some of the country's leading clubs being beaten by small teams in the Welsh Cup.

The strength of Welsh club rugby is also reflected in the fact that only Welsh club sides have ever been considered strong enough to take on overseas touring teams. Cardiff, Llanelli, Swansea and Newport have all beaten the New Zealand All Blacks.

The Americas

Argentina

Argentina is probably the strongest rugby playing country in the Americas. The game was introduced there by the large numbers of British engineers working on the railways. Although club matches have been played since 1873 it was not until 1949 that the first international match, against France, was played. Since then Argentina has beaten most of the major countries at the sport and have also recorded a draw against New Zealand.

Canada

The vast size of Canada has been a handicap to the growth of the game. The three main areas where rugby is played are British Columbia in the West, Manitoba in the Centre and the Maritime Provinces in the East. It was not until 1929 that Canada had its own Rugby Union. The first tour by a Canadian team was in 1902 and they won about half of their matches in Britain. Since then teams from New Zealand, Italy, Japan and England have toured Canada. More locally there is an annual fixture against the USA in which Canada

Wales is famous for being a great rugby-playing country. The 1988 Welsh team won the Triple Crown competition.

The 1988 Canadian team on tour in Ireland.

has a narrow lead in the number of victories won. Canada has recently developed its coaching schemes on a national basis and has encouraged more schools and junior teams to take up rugby.

Asia

Japan

The game was played at the end of the nineteenth century at Keji University and developed through both schools and universities. The Japanese RFU was formed in 1926 and now governs over 3000 clubs in the country. Although extremely successful against other Asian countries their lack of size has been a disadvantage against the major rugby nations.

Other Asian countries

The game flourishes in Hong Kong and Malaysia and is also expanding in India, China and Sri Lanka.

Africa

South Africa

One of the leading countries in world rugby, South Africa has been isolated for some thirty years because the South African government runs a system of racial separation, known as 'apartheid'. Although black, Asian as well as white people now have the chance of representing their country, most rugby playing countries refuse to play South Africa because of the apartheid system.

Rugby was first played in Cape Town in 1875 between British soldiers stationed there. A British side toured South Africa in 1891 winning all its matches but by 1896 the standard of rugby had so improved they beat the British Isles in the last test. Ten years later South Africa had arrived as a leading rugby playing country. Since that date only New Zealand has had any regular success against them. South African amateur rugby players have toured abroad and were known as the 'Springboks', named after a South African type of antelope.

Zimbabwe

Formerly known as Rhodesia, Zimbabwe has always had a large European population and they brought the game to the country in 1890. In 1895 the Rhodesian RFU was formed but was renamed the Zimbabwean RFU in 1980. Zimbabwe

The South African team are known as the Springboks. Most countries refuse to play South Africa at rugby because of apartheid.

rugby was helped to flourish because they competed in the South African Currie Cup, and several of their players represented South Africa. The country has always attracted touring teams as club rugby is not as strong as it was, and the Zimbabweans rely upon touring club sides to provide the real challenge.

Australasia

Australia

Rugby union is mainly played in the two states of Queensland and New South Wales. There is much competition for players from both rugby league and Australian rules. The game came to Australia in 1840 through Sydney University and in 1882 a New South Wales side toured New Zealand. The first full Australian side played New Zealand in 1903. Despite the other two codes there are over 300 clubs in Australia. It was Australia who brought about the change in the laws so that a player could only kick directly into touch inside their own '22' which has done much to make the game faster to play and more exciting to watch. The international touring rugby union football team of Australia are known as the 'Wallabies' named after a Kangaroo-type of animal found in Australia.

Fiji

It was the military who introduced the game to Fiji in the 1880s but it was not until 1913 that the Fijian's Rugby Union was formed. Their first international was against Western Samoa in 1924. Since 1945 the Fijians have toured Europe, Australia and New Zealand thrilling crowds with their fast open attacking rugby.

New Zealand

Rugby has been played in New Zealand since 1870. The game quickly became popular and at the formation of the New Zealand RFU in 1892 there were over 700 clubs in existence. Now there are over 11,000 clubs. Early football in New Zealand was a mixture of association, rugby and Australian rules. In 1915 the original All Blacks toured Great Britain losing only to Wales out of their thirty-three

matches. In 1888/9 a Maori side toured Britain playing seventy-four matches, losing only twenty-one of them. In 1922 the Maori Rugby Union fully integrated with the New Zealand RFU.

New Zealand's game is traditionally based upon powerful forward play and secondary phase possession. The structure in New Zealand is perhaps the best in the world with some fifteen grades of competition from children to adults.

The New Zealand team, known as the All Blacks, perform their famous Maori Haka war dance.

Tonga

The game did not arrive in Tonga until 1923 and the oldest club only goes back to 1939. Now there are over seventy-eight clubs from which a lively national team is produced. Their oldest rivals are Fiji. They also play Western Samoa and have toured Australia, New Zealand and the British Isles.

Of the older countries in this area, Western Samoa is a formidable force and recently won the Pacific Championships. Tonga, Cook Islands and the Solomon Islands play inter-island matches.

Famous teams and players

In rugby, touring clubs consisting of the very top professionals, are an intricate part of the game. These clubs have no base, but play several matches a season, on tours. Membership of them is a much-coveted honour and is only acquired by invitation from the club's committee.

Barbarians (Ba-Bas) (Britain)

This famous club with their black and white hooped jerseys are closely associated with attractive running rugby. Until recently they had five traditional fixtures: Cardiff, Swansea, Leicester and the East Midlands, Penarth and Newport but Penarth has now been replaced by a touring side. Such is the reputation of the club that traditionally the last fixture of any tour is against the Barbarians.

   The Club was started by W.P. Carpmore, the former Blackheath player and Cambridge Blue, at Bradford in 1890. Players invited are often internationals but many non-internationals have been invited too. The Barbarians also tour abroad and have visited Australia, New Zealand and Canada.

British Lions (Britain)

The British Lions consist of players from the British Isles, and regularly make tours of Australia, New Zealand and South Africa. The first official Lions Tour was in 1910 when they toured South Africa, although British Isles teams have been going abroad since 1888. With long sea journeys each way these tours could last up to seven or eight months. This restricted selection as many players were unable to spare the time to be away for such a long period. Success at test level was limited with only one series being won against both South Africa and New Zealand. In Australia the Lions have had more success, so far winning all three series.

All Blacks (New Zealand)

The New Zealand All Blacks are held in very high esteem throughout the world. The first national New Zealand team

The All Blacks celebrate yet another victory.

was formed in 1893 to tour Australia. The All Blacks went on their first major overseas tour in 1905 to Britain, France and North America, winning thirty-four out of thirty-five matches. Since then they have consistently dominated world rugby and by 1988, out of the 1,000 matches they had played, they had lost only 100. They won the first World Cup held in 1987.

Wallabies (Australia)

The Australian Rugby Union was not founded until 1949, although the first national Australian team was formed in 1899 and beat Britain 13–3. For many years Australian rules

The Wallabies gather round for a pep talk before play.

and rugby league were more widely played in Australia than rugby union. However, since 1980 rugby union has grown substantially with increased sponsorship and crowd attendance. In the 1987 World Cup Australia reached the semi-finals losing to France 24–30.

Famous players

Dusty Hare (England)

Dusty Hare, a former England full-back, is the record points scorer in rugby union history. He has scored over 6,000 points. He became England's most capped full-back with 25 appearances but retired from international rugby in 1984.

Dusty Hare (England) is one of the most prolific goal kickers of all time.

Dean Richards (England)

The England number eight won his first cap for England against Ireland in 1986, and scored two tries in that match. He is considered a good line-out player and plays well both in attack and in covering ground in defence. He scored against Japan in the 1987 World Cup.

Gareth Edwards (Wales)

Gareth Edwards played fifty-three times in succession for Wales as scrum-half. At the age of 20 years 7 months he became the youngest captain of Wales. He has scored more tries than any other scrum-half in world rugby. He retired in 1978.

J P R Williams (Wales)

J P R Williams is the world's most capped full-back with fifty-four caps. He was also a successful tennis player winning Junior Wimbledon in 1966. In rugby he won a record number of Grand Slam titles, a total of three in 1971, 1976 and 1978.

Andy Irvine (Scotland)

Andy Irvine, a former Scotland full-back, has scored more points in international rugby than any other player; over 300! He holds the world record for a full-back, of ten tries, and he is Scotland's most capped player with 60 caps.

Gavin Hastings (Scotland)

Gavin Hastings was an outstanding schoolboy rugby player. He won his first cap for Scotland against France in 1986. That season he set a new Scottish record by scoring fifty-two points in the Five Nations Championships. In only his tenth international against France in the 1987 World Cup, he took his points total to over 100. As a full-back he is a good tackler, a fast runner and a powerful kicker with either foot.

Colin Meads (New Zealand)

Lock-forward and former captain, Colin Meads is the greatest New Zealand rugby player ever, with a record fifty-five caps and over 133 appearances between 1957 and 1971.

Hugo Porta (Argentina)

Hugo Porta, the Argentinian fly-half, is the most prolific scorer in international rugby history. He appeared for Argentina over forty times, making his debut against Romania in 1973. His world record points total is 359 in forty matches.

Mark Ella (Australia)

Mark Ella captained the Australian Wallabies on their tour of Britain in 1982. As fly-half his abilities were in taking possession well, handling the ball skilfully, reading the game accurately and instinctively linking between backs and forwards.

Hugo Porta (Argentina) one of the great fly-halves in the world passes the ball down the line.

Mike Gibson (Ireland)

Mike Gibson is the world's most capped player. He played in sixty-nine internationals for Ireland and another twelve for the British Isles giving a total of eighty-one (one more than the great Willie John McBride). He began as a fly-half and then became a centre.

Phil Orr (Ireland) has the bulky physique necessary to give him the strength to be a great prop.

Phil Orr (Ireland)

Phil Orr was first capped in 1976 and toured New Zealand with the British Lions a year later. He is one of the best props of all time and was selected by Ireland forty-one times in succession. He eventually was capped over fifty times.

Jean Pierre-Rives (France)

Jean Pierre-Rives is France's most capped flanker with a total of forty-seven caps between 1975 and 1984; thirty of them were as captain which is another record. He was a great skirmisher for the ball; if you looked out for his blonde hair, you were sure to know where the action was.

Serge Blanco (France)

Serge Blanco is reputed to be the top full-back in the world. His finest moment was when he scored the winning try for France in the 1987 World Cup semi-final against Australia.

Serge Blanco (France)
takes a high leap as he kicks.

Eric Champ (France)

Eric Champ is a flank forward to rival France's previous great flanker, Jean Pierre-Rives. He won his first cap for France in 1985 and by 1988 he had already won twenty-two caps. By the end of his career he could quite easily double that figure.

Eric Champ (France) has the strength and speed needed to be an excellent forward.

Famous grounds

Twickenham

Twickenham has been the home of English rugby since 1910. It was once a market garden and is often referred to as 'Billy William's Cabbage Patch', and it covers an area of thirty acres. Spectators are restricted to 62,000, most of them seated and under cover. The most modern part of the ground is the South Stand which was opened in 1981.

Twickenham is the home of English rugby.

Cardiff Arms Park

Cardiff Arms Park is one of the most modern grounds in the world, capable of holding some 74,000 spectators. For many years the Arms Park had shared all Welsh home fixtures with Swansea, but this changed in 1954 when Cardiff was allocated all home fixtures. To raise money to help cover the cost the Welsh Rugby Union issued debenture shares of £50 and £100 which entitles the holder to receive one or two tickets respectively for every international match.

Murrayfield

Murrayfield has been the home of Scottish rugby since 1925, and was the first rugby ground to invest in an underground heating system, which has produced an excellent playing surface whatever the weather conditions. In 1915 for the Scotland v Wales encounter, the world's largest crowd (over 104,000) were admitted. Safety limits on grounds will now ensure that such a figure is not reached again.

A rugby ground

Key

1 Halfway line
2 10m line
3 22m line
4 Goal line
5 Dead ball line
6 Lineout line
7 Goal posts
8 Touch judges
9 Advertising billboards
10 Floodlights
11 Electronic scoreboard
12 Video surveillance equipment
13 TV stand
14 Line flags

Eden Park, Auckland is one of New Zealand's best Test grounds.

Eden Park Auckland

Eden Park is the second largest ground in New Zealand and has been used for rugby tests since 1921. It is also one of New Zealand's famous cricket grounds and has a capacity of over 57,000.

Sydney Cricket Ground

Sydney Cricket Ground has been in use since 1852, primarily as a sports ground for troops. In 1878 it was opened up to the general public and since then lawn tennis, rugby league, soccer, cricket and Australian rules football have been played there. It was also the site for the Empire Games when they took place in Australia. The crowd capacity is limited to 52,000. It is a ground of contrasts as many of the older buildings remain but are dwarfed by giant video screens and floodlight towers.

Loftus Versveld, in South Africa, has a huge capacity of 65,000.

Clothes and equipment

Pride in your appearance has much to do with how you play. A well turned out fifteen always seems to start a match with an advantage – but this was not always the case. In early games no special kit was worn. Players simply took off their jacket and caps. However, players began to wear specially made boots. Hacking, the kicking of your opponent's legs beneath him, was allowed and therefore boots were adapted to provide the most damaging hack.

Dress progress was slow and in 1871 the accepted lower dress was long cricket flannels tucked into your socks. The first shorts used came below the knees and it was not until the 1930s they appeared above them.

It was not until the 1960s that it was accepted that lightweight clothing and boots could assist players to play more effectively. Boots are light with padded ankle support. The uppers are made of leather and the soles plastic. Studs by law have to be safety ones and are limited in length to

(Below) The modern rugby boot is made of synthetic materials and has safety studs to prevent nasty injuries.

(Left) Rugby clothes need to be hard wearing and easy to wash. These young players' kit takes a hammering when they play in muddy conditions.

The modern rugby ball is made of nitro-laminate material to suit all weather and pitch conditions.

18mm. Shirts are made of hardwearing cotton or cotton/viscose fabric. Shorts are of cotton satin drill and designed so that they do not interfere with movement.

Socks and shinguards are generally made of synthetic materials. Most socks are nylon which do not become heavy and uncomfortable in bad weather. Shinguards are light and designed to fit the shape of the leg. A more modern trend is that most players now wear gum shields in their mouths for added protection.

The Ball

The unique shape of the rugby ball stems from the use of a pig's bladder in the early days of rugby. This could vary in size and was easily split. The Gilbert family, who were boot and shoemakers for Rugby School, then encased the bladder in four panels of leather. It was inflated by lung power through the stem of a clay pipe. Around 1880 a rubber bladder was used and also a primitive pump for inflating it. In wet weather the ball got heavier and heavier as well as more slippery. Now specially treated leather balls are used but mitro-laminate materials and vulcanised rubber balls are used at all levels. Their high grip and waterproof surface ensure the game does not suffer because of weather conditions.

Goals

The goals comprise of two upright posts of not less than 11ft (3.35m) which are 18ft 6in (5.64m) apart with a crossbar 10ft (3.05m) from the ground.

The goal posts at Twickenham have been the crucial targets in deciding the outcome of many matches.

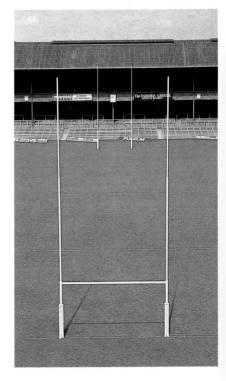

Fitness and training

Fitness

To play rugby successfully and to the best of your ability you must be fit, and that means match fitness. Getting fit is hard work. Ways of achieving match fitness are a combination of the following: circuit training – interval running – weight training.

Circuit training

This is a progressive method of achieving complete physical fitness. It has the advantage that an individual may set his own programme. A typical circuit may consist of:

- 20 step-ups
- 10 press-ups
- 10 squat jumps
- 10 trunk curls
- 25 metre monkey run
- Spring plus two forward rolls
- 10 press-ups
- 25 metre crab walk

Remember that because you are young, you may be fit, but you are not match fit; that takes time and effort.

Rory Underwood (England) uses interval running and circuit training to help in his fitness training.

Interval running

This is ideal for speed, stamina and recovery. One of the biggest problems a player has to combat is that of fatigue. In interval running a player alternates between jogging and flat-out running. As you become fitter you will increase the flat-out runs gradually until they reach a maximum of 100 to 150 m. To add interest to interval running you can incorporate the following six variations which will not only improve your fitness but also improve your basic skills:

1 Fifty metre sprint during which, two dummies, two sidesteps and one swerve is performed.
2 Jog trot dribbling a ball for 400 m.
3 Dribbling a little more quickly, practise three or four pick-ups over 100 m.
4 Over a 400 m run, punt ball high in air and catch some five times, grubber kick along ground and pick up five times i.e. run – punt and catch – run – grubber kick and pick-up – run – punt and catch etc.
5 25 m sprint with two hand offs with alternate hands.
6 Throwing the ball high in the air in front of you, taking one or two paces, jumping and taking ball high in the air with two hands.

Training and coaching are important at all levels. Here the England team use a scrummage machine to build up their strength in the scrum.

Weight training

All players need strength and this can be improved at home as well as in the gym. You do not need to spend a lot of money on weights or dumb-bells. For weights you can use iron bars with bags of sand at the end and, for dumb-bells, sand-filled plastic bottles.

1 Hold the bar in both hands, lift your shoulders towards your ears, press back as far as possible, then return to starting position.

2 Hold the bar about shoulder width apart, and raise it to chin by lifting the elbows high and keeping bar near to body.

3 With dumb-bells in hand, arms down by sides – lift sideways as high as possible.

4 With dumb-bells in hand arms down by side – raise arms forward to directly above head. Keep arms straight.

5 Feet apart with dumb-bell resting on shoulder behind the neck. Bend forwards keeping legs straight until body is parallel to the floor. Raise your trunk back to an upright position. Keep chin up throughout the exercise.

Do the first exercise twice, the second three times and so on. After a few sessions you can start to increase the number of times you do each exercise.

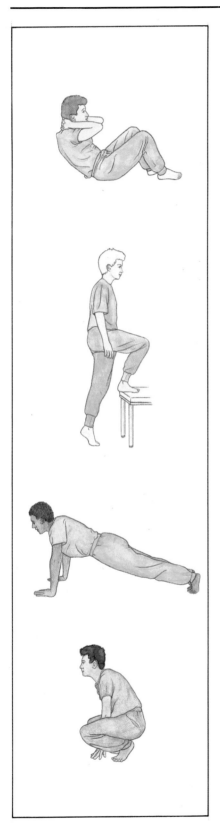

Physical exercises

1 Trunk curls
Lie on back, bend knees, hands behind neck. Raise shoulders and back off the ground. Look up to help keep back straight.

2 Forward roll
A type of somersault – dive forward, hands touch ground a shoulder's width apart – somersault with legs together. Do not use hands to assist to return to upright position. Head must not touch ground.

3 Monkey run
Squat on ground with hands and feet all touching. Run along with body weight mainly on hands.

4 Step-up
Use a bench or chair. Step up on to it – then step down.

5 Press-ups
Put hands on ground, arms straight, body fully extended behind. Bend arms until chest and trunk are just touching the ground, then straighten arms, keep trunk parallel to ground during both raising and lowering – Don't sag!

6 Squat jumps
Crouch position with fingers resting lightly on ground between feet. Jump as high as you can extending arms vertically and returning to crouch position.

7 Crab walk
Sit on ground – hands behind. Press and raise body off ground. Take weight on hands and feet and move along backwards.

It is only by following an intensive training routine with complete dedication, that rugby players can reach a peak fitness condition. The very top professionals have to be extremely fit. (Opposite) David Kirk, captain of New Zealand, receives the trophy after the All Blacks won the 1987 World Cup.

Skills and tactics

Passing – taking a pass

Rugby is primarily a handling game and giving and receiving passes are the most common events on a rugby field. Passing for forwards is not necessarily the same as for backs. Often in close passing the player will not have the room or time to do textbook passes. As long as the ball gets to the next player it does not matter how it is done.

When in the open a player must pass correctly. This is the one that transfers the ball by the quickest possible method to the next player and in such a way that he will collect it at top speed. To achieve this you will need to hold the ball correctly:

1 Hold the ball in two hands with grip coming from the fingers
2 Fingers must be splayed
3 Ball tilted slightly towards you
4 Arms are straight

A stand up scrum - half pass.

For a pass to the right:
1 Arms will come across the body to the left – at the farthest point the wrists will automatically turn over so that the ball is now tilting forward
2 The right leg will now be forwards and while the weight is still on that leg the arms will be brought across the body and at the same time the body will turn towards the receiver of the pass

3 The ball will be released just before reaching the end of the return swing, with a final thrust from the fingers and wrists

Remember:
- Always pass off the opposite foot to the direction of the pass, i.e. for a pass to the left off the right foot
- Pass in front of the receiver so that he can take the ball at top speed
- Look where you are passing

(Left) The orthodox pass. Notice the passer looking when he is passing and falling away as he delivers the pass.

Receiving the pass

Ideally you take and give a pass in one movement. The main point is speed.

1 Keep your eyes on the ball
2 For a pass from the left, hands will go to the left
3 Do not snatch at the ball

Beating a player

The next natural sequence, now that you are running with the ball is to be able to beat an opponent with the ball in your hands. The ways of doing this are by dummy, sidestep, swerve, jerk , hand off and variations of pace.

The dummy

This is simply pretending to pass:

1 You must go through all the motions of giving the pass but without actually releasing the ball
2 The quick stab towards the receiver will deceive no one

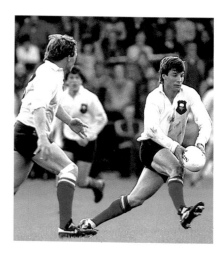

(Below) Rob Andrew, the England fly-half, executes the dummy which is simply pretending to pass.

The sidestep (to the right)

1 Run straight at the tackler
2 Slam you left foot into the ground with all your weight on the inside of that foot
3 Thrust your right foot over and nearly parallel to the left one
4 Bring your left foot up and past the right and carry on in the new direction.

For a sidestep to the left, reverse points 2 to 4. Remember a sidestep automatically slows up your run, so you must accelerate immediately afterwards.

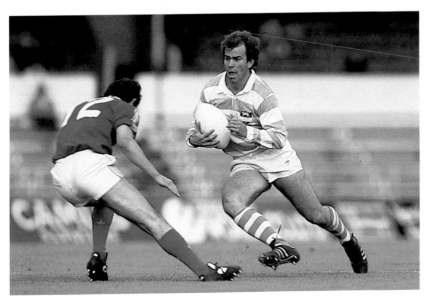

The sidestep. Notice how Madero of Argentina thrusts off his left foot.

The swerve

This is the most natural way to get round an opponent. The secret is to run on the outside of the foot the way you want to swerve. For a swerve to the right, lean that way; put the weight on the outside of your right foot and the next step with the right foot in the new direction.

Variation of pace

Perhaps the most deceptive of all ploys. It is not just simply increasing or decreasing speed but the ability to alter the length of your stride. If you are running just below your top speed as the tackler prepares to launch himself, you accelerate or lengthen your stride. This will cause him to misjudge the distance and the tackle.

Remember, when running with the ball, you are trying to make the would be tackler:

1 Hesitate
2 Get off balance – so creating a gap. When created accelerate out of it

Having varied his pace to deceive his opponents, Rory Underwood (England) then accelerates his stride.

The hand-off

A most effective way of beating your opponent especially when combined with the swerve. Keep the ball in both hands until the moment before you hand off.
Do not slacken pace and then:
1 Transfer ball into one arm
2 Use the heel of the palm
3 Straighten the arm just before impact
4 Do it forcefully
5 As soon as hand off completed get the ball back into two hands

Kicking the punt

Kicking the punt will be used in

1 Defence: kicking straight into touch
2 Attack: alternatives – diagram kick, cross kick, up and under, short kick ahead and grubber.

There are far more attacking than defensive kicks. For all the kicks the mechanism is the same:

1 Hold the ball in two hands with one hand at the bottom of one side and the other hand on the top of the ball.
2 Push the ball down
3 Kicking leg must be straight
4 Keep head well down – on point of contact and follow through
5 Keep the toe pointed.

The art of kicking lies in the timing.

Remember when kicking for touch it is better to kick 10 m into touch, than 30 m with the ball still in play. Most important learn to kick with either foot.

Huw Davies (England) prepares to kick the punt. Note the position of his hands.

Catching the ball

There will be many occasions when you have to field the ball from a kick. The catching process is simple enough. The difficulty lies in being under the ball when it comes down. It is easier to run forwards than to run backwards. Once you have judged the flight of the ball and are now underneath it, it is important to keep

1 Eyes on the ball
2 One foot slightly forward
3 Arms bent – hands at head level, but in front of you
4 As the ball touches hands, guide it to the chest
5 Keep elbows close to the side of the body

Gavin Hastings (Scotland) kicks strongly with both feet. Here he is about kick with his left foot.

Drop kick

This kick is a variation of the punt, but this time you kick the ball just after it has hit the ground.

1 The ball drops straight down leaning slightly towards you
2 It bounces just opposite and slightly in front of the non-kicking foot
3 Aim to kick the ball on the rebound
4 Keep head down and weight is now on non-kicking foot
5 Follow through as for punt

Place kick

A good place kicker is invaluable. Make a mark in the ground in which to position the ball. This is done by using your heel. Some players prefer to make heel marks towards each other, so that the ball is raised off the ground.

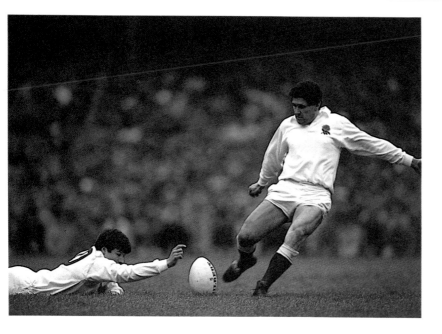

Marcus Rose (England) takes a place kick which is held in position for him by another player.

Main points

1 Having placed the ball, measure out your run-up
2 Before the commencement of your run up look at where you are aiming to kick the ball
3 Keep your kicking leg straight – point of impact at bottom of the swing
4 Body leaning forward on point of impact
5 Follow through, keeping head down all the time. Don't be tempted to look up too quickly to see whether you have kicked the goal

Dribbling and falling

1 The dribble must be done at speed.
2 To achieve maximum control:
   - Dribble with inside of feet
   - Knees bent a little outwards
   - Body will be slightly over the ball
   - Keep ball as near as possible to the foot

Should the ball bounce up, grab it with both hands. To stop a dribble an opposing player has to fall on the ball. You should try and stop the dribble as soon as possible. The longer you leave it the harder it becomes. Dive over the ball with your back to the dribbler and gather the ball into your body, then get up immediately.

Tackling

Of all the essentials, the one that can be the most satisfying is tackling. To succeed it must be performed correctly. The tackle although a defensive move can be the launching point of a counter attack. All players must be able to tackle. There are four basic types of tackle: from the side, from behind, head on and the smother. If at all possible, manoeuvre yourself so that you are tackling from the side. It is the easiest of the tackles, and if performed correctly, the ball may go loose or the pass go astray.

The smother tackle can prevent a pass being given but it must not be used as an excuse for high tackling. You have to bring the opponent with the ball to the ground. This requires you to go in hard, with your shoulder aiming to hit the runner between his hips and knees.

At the other extremes the neck or head tackle is illegal and going for your opponent's chest or waist means he can hand you off far more easily. Your shoulder will knock your opponent off balance and by anchoring their thighs or knees they will be unable to regain it.

Remember not to hesitate; take off hard; aim to hit your opponent between the hips and knees with your shoulder. Position your head to the side and behind the runner with the ball. Their backside should act as your cushion. Lock your arms round their thighs. Recover quickly, as the ball will go loose and you want possession.

The tackler manages to get a good hold on the player with the ball.

Rory Underwood (England) on the receiving end of an excellent front tackle.

Tackling from behind. The tackler dives at his opponent from about one metre away.

Front tackle

Always move towards your opponent with the ball, but in the tackle don't try to hit them backwards. Get your feet and body to the side of your opponent and grasp them firmly round the thighs. Remember to keep your head to one side.

Tackle from behind

When someone makes a break and you are covering from behind, if you have the speed to overtake your opponent with the ball, you are then in the position to make a good tackle. As the runner cushions your tackle, it is not as difficult as it looks. When you are about a metre from your opponent, dive as for the side tackle and put your head to one side. Again point of aim will be just below the hips.

Smother tackle

The smother tackle should only be used when it is essential not to let a pass be given. Tackling is a vital and essential part of the game – memorise the vital points and remember never to shadow tackle.

Full-back

The full-back is often referred to as the last line of defence, but in modern rugby they should be the first instrument of counter attack. A full-back must be a master of these essentials:
- Catching the ball
- Kicking with either foot
- Tackling
- Collecting a rolling ball
- Falling

A full-back must be prepared to practise, and practise again at all these essentials. The full-back's position in depth behind the threequarter line will depend upon the kicking ability of your opponents. Remember, it is much easier to run forward than backward to field the ball. When you field the ball you always have two alternatives: to kick for touch or to run and open up the game.

Gavin Hastings (Scotland) an excellent full-back, is tackled by Richard Moriarty (Wales).

Wing three-quarter

At one time the wing three-quarters were reckoned to be the fastest players in the side and the leading try scorers. In the modern game, speed is still vital, they do score tries but their defensive qualities are much called upon as they are often used as a second full-back. In consequence a wing three-quarter must master:
- Giving and taking a pass
- Tackling
- Swerve, sidestep, dummy, change of pace
- Kicking
- Tackling
- Falling

The wing three-quarter will have three main weapons in his armoury, the sidestep, swerve and change of pace. There are going to be times when he will have to kick. These kicks have to be constructive and usually there are three options open to him:

1 The short kick ahead over the waiting tackler's head and the winger either running round to catch the ball or dribble it on
2 The longer kick in which the winger reckons to outpace the opposition to the ball

3 The cross kick

All wingers should put in plenty of practice at these three types as they can lead to tries being scored. In defence the winger must also do everything at speed. His speed will be invaluable in defence as he will be able to corner flag. He is in fact one of three full-backs in his team. He must give the rest of his team confidence either to finish off an attacking movement or to cover in defence. Remember that you need to be a versatile player.

John Kirwan (New Zealand), a winger, under considerable pressure from the French in the 1987 World Cup final.

The centre three-quarter

A centre has three main tasks: in attack, to make openings and to move the ball quickly to the wing; in defence, to break down the opposition's three-quarter attacks. A centre must also possess an eye for an opening and be tough and resilient.

Centres should run at a slight diagonal because this puts them in a better position to give a pass, to use the inside break, to go for a gap and so draw two players and change direction more violently. Never run across the field as this crowds the rest of your three-quarter line. A centre will vary his tactics. It is no good just passing the ball on and saying, 'Now you do something with it!' A centre can make the break in three ways:

Outside break: here the centre relies upon acceleration and swerve

Inside break: this is often made by using the sidestep to take you inside your opponent. But having gone through the gap you must swing outwards again to avoid running into covering forwards.

Half break: often the most effective break of all. With the half break you are going for a gap between two players, causing them to converge towards you. When both are fully committed you send your pass out to the next player who will go straight through the gap created.

In all breaks you must take the ball on the burst.

Centres will be involved in many passing movements and to keep the momentum going they must always pass in front of their opponent. Centres must also be able to kick. This should be the last, not first option. They must remember that by kicking they are giving away possession and therefore they must kick accurately in attack if possession is to be regained.

Michael Lynagh (Australia), an outside half, renowned for his magnificent kicking skills.

Fly-half or outside-half

The fly-half is the pivot of a team's attack and defence. Fly-halves must be able to handle the ball well; be able to move the ball quickly and accurately; be accurate kickers with both feet; be quick off the mark; tackle well; read a game;

spot an opening and know whether to pass or kick.

The fly-half and scrum-half work closely together. For scrummages, rucks, mauls and lineouts the fly-half will receive the pass from the scrum-half. To get the three-quarter line moving fly-halves must take the ball at speed and in front of themselves if this is to be achieved. Lots of practice will be necessary. The fly-halves will run diagonally after receiving the ball, so as to take themselves away from the breaking forwards. They must remember to straighten up as soon as possible, if they are to give themselves all the attacking options possible. Successful fly-halves vary their mode of attack.

A fly-half must keep the game flowing – if there is no gap to exploit then the ball must be passed immediately it is received. If the fly-half does make a break the pass must be made as soon as possible.

Jonathan Davis (Wales), a great fly-half, gets the three-quarter line moving.

Scrum-half

The scrum-half is a vital position and one which demands many qualities including good physical fitness. The scrum-half must be robust, nimble and quick thinking and able to pass quickly either way. The scrum-half is the link between the forwards and backs and decides how possession is used;

The Australian scrum-half releases the ball from the scrum. He will pass to the fly-half so that the backs can go on attack.

therefore a great tactical awareness is necessary. Passes can either be diving or standing up and should be done so that they give a quick, long and accurate pass.

Accuracy is required to get the backs moving, so the scrum half will pass in front of the fly-half to enable the ball to be taken on the burst. The halves must understand what the other is likely to do. These are the two passes a scrum-half will be likely to use:

Stand up pass: For a pass to the right from a scrum or ruck, the scrum-half will need to stay close to the forwards. As the ball comes out of the scrum, the scrum-half's left foot will be positioned near the ball and the right foot a yard or so away. With knees well bent the scrum-half will pick up and pass in one flowing movement – the arms must be kept straight.

Dive Pass: Again it is essential for the scrum-half to be close to the scrum or ruck and to pick up the ball turn and dive pass in one movement. It is up to the fly-half to make any variations in pace or position, to ensure that the scrum-half arrives in the right place at the right time to take the pass. Scrum-halves must also be accurate punters of the ball. In attack they can get the opposition running backwards by kicking over the forward's head. In defence they may decide that a direct kick to touch will be safer than getting the ball back to the fly-half.

This view of a scrum shows the scrum-half about to put the ball into the scrum.

Prop

There are two props in the rugby pack, a tight-head and a loose-head, both of which are important specialist positions. Physically you need to be strong with good upper body strength and sturdy legs.

The loose head prop needs to be a master of the basic techniques of scrummaging with firm feet positions, a flat back, tight binding and eyes open. The prop must have the ability to use legs, hips and back to drive upwards and leave a clear path and view for the hooker. The tight-head prop must also be a master of the basic scrummaging essentials and must be built to stand the compression that is experienced in the set scrum. You support the front and middle jumpers in the line-out and wrestle in all phases of support play.

Hooker

The hooker is the middle player in the front row of the scrum whose job is to hook the ball back in a set scrum. You must have flexible hips and be able to twist your striking leg into rather improbable positions. A quick reflex action is required if you are to get the ball on the put-in. Good binding of the front row is essential. The hooker should always bind over the top of the shoulders of the two props putting you closer to the middle of the tunnel.

Another important job for today's hooker is throwing in the ball at the line-out. It is essential to throw in accurately and to do this you must have (for a righthanded thrower – the opposite for a left):

- Left leg slightly forward
- Ball resting in palm of hand
- Non-throwing hand steadies the ball
- Bring hand back above the head so that the player's eyes are in line with it
- Little finger touches lace on ball
- In follow through – throwing hand follows the ball

The locks

The locks are the powerhouse of the scrum and the leading jumpers in the line-out. The locks must maintain a flat back with feet back, a raised chin and a strong tight binding. To

The front row of the scrum, the props and the hooker, prepare to go down into the scrum position.

The locks jump to gain possession of the ball.

transmit the best shove the locks will push with their shoulders against the top of the thighs. Strong tight binding is also necessary to stop the front row splitting.

The line-out too, is an important area for the locks. They must not only have the ability to win ball in the line-out, but also be able to deny or spoil the opposition's line-out ball.

Locks are usually large in physique and their role in set play, rucks, mauls and support play makes great demands on their strength and stamina. Even though they are larger and heavier than most of the team, they are expected to reach breakdowns quickly.

Flanker

The flanker needs to have aggressive tackling and the ablity to gain or regain the ball and then distribute it. A flanker must have the art to instinctively secure the ball on the ground. You must have quick acceleration as well as pace to get to the breakdown or to support another member of the team. In support you need to be a good mauler. Flankers have an important job in the line-out and must be able to jump and catch the ball.

Number eight

Control at the base of the scrum is the most important job of the number eight. You must have tactical sense, knowing

The number eight holds the locks together and provides the final thrust of the scrum.

Findlay Calder (Scotland) a great flanker, has taken possession of the ball and accelerates quickly.

when to release the ball quickly, when to hold the ball and when to call on a variety of backrow moves, always being in communication with the scrum half.

You need to have a physical presence, which will be invaluable in the line-out. The strength of this physical presence is also required in the scrummage, to bind the locks together and then to give the concerted shove required. It is one of the most demanding positions on the field requiring: spirit, fitness, stamina, speed and intelligence.

Fitting individual skills into unit skills

Backs in attack

From all set pieces the forwards initially should be tied up, giving the three-quarters time and space in which to set up a penetrative attack. As a three-quarter you must decide the options open to you – they are likely to be the following:
• The ball going down the three-quarter line to the wing
• Someone in the three-quarter line makes a break
• Someone in the three-quarter line does an attacking kick
Passing the ball quickly down the wing is one of the most effective ways of testing the opposition.

To get a three-quarter line moving at speed the backs must align themselves in such a way that they take the ball at speed. This will mean lying back at least forty-five degrees from the fly-half and anything up to eighty degrees.

Normally three-quarters are spaced three to five metres apart, but by varying this spacing you can set up some interesting attacking moves. You can have the fly-half and inside-centre closer together and the outside-centre and winger ten to fifteen metres apart. This will cause the defence to vary their spacing so that they cover their opposite numbers. The attacking fly-half and inside-centre must run straight, and just before the ball is about to be passed to the outside-centre, will veer away to the right. As you receive the ball you must aim for the gap between the outside-centre and the wing. This will cause your opposite centre and also the opposite wing to close in towards you. As you head into the gap you must give a long pass to your wing who should now be in position to overlap. Gaps can also be created by the three-quarter line missing out a player in their passing movement. This enables the ball to reach the wing more

One of the great centres, Philippe Sella (France), keeps the attack going.

quickly and gives more room in which to move. When a set piece takes place in the centre of the field the three-quarter line will split. The initiative will be taken by the side with the ball. The opposing three-quarters make sure they are marking their opposite numbers.

Backs in defence

Although three-quarters are regarded as the attacking unit of a team, they are also a major defence one. They are involved in more open play than most. Mistakes are costly and usually everyone can see them. There are four basic rules for three-quarters to remember in defence:
- Come up in formation so as to leave no gaps
- Go in hard upon the attacking threequarter
- Tackle your opposite number when he has the ball (in other words no shadow tackling)
- Get back into position quickly

At the line-out the three-quarters must stay ten metres back until the line-out is over. It is essential that the fly-half controls the alignment of the three-quarters and that they keep their eye upon him/her.

Forwards in attack

The main object of any pack is to get possession. When they have possession they must keep it. They must either use it themselves or release the ball to their three-quarters. To attack the forwards must get possession of the ball and this requires a thorough knowledge of the mechanics of scrummaging. Once the hooker has the ball, it will be released to the three-quarters or the forwards, who will initiate the attack themselves. This can be done by wheeling and dribbling.

The dribble is often more effective if the ball is picked up as soon as you are in the open, and you have the choice of interpassing with the forwards or linking up with the three-quarters. Attacking moves by the backrow can also be used to set up an attack from the scrum. These moves should be as simple as possible and should have options.

One attacking move which can bring immediate and positive results, is the pushover try. This will start with a five metre scrummage near the opposition try line. The attacking pack should go for an upward lift of the opposition front row. The ball should then be held by the number eight just in front, in order to detach and touch down as soon as the ball crosses the line.

The line-out

If the forwards are to launch a successful attack from the line-out, they must either catch the ball cleanly or 'guide' the ball accurately to a backing up player. 'Tapping' back is usually fraught with danger. When the ball is caught the catcher must release it at the top of the jump or bring the ball down immediately.

The catcher must receive support from the rest of the forwards. This will require binding so that the opposition are unable to break through. If the opposition pack are more intent upon spoiling your possession then it will be possible for the catcher's pack to drive through the line-out and by short interpassing make ground. They can drive until stopped and then maul or ruck the ball backwards to their scrum-half. The latter will cause the opposition to have their forwards sucked into the ruck allowing the attacking three-quarters more room in which to move.

Peeling is an effective form of forward attack. This is where players leave the line-out to attack around the extremes of it. The peel can be from the front or end of the line-out and a link up with the backs may or may not be used – in brief, options are kept open. If the peel is around the back and the ball is initially thrown to the number six who needs an 'umbrella' of players to guide the ball down to; do

A lineout in progress. Note how the front two players peel round in support.

The Argentinian forwards in blue and white striped shirts, primarily try to gain possession of the ball; but failing that they must block any break away attack that their opponents, the Italian team, may try to make.

not expect the number six to pinpoint the ball down to just one player.

Forwards in defence

You should read this section with the idea of immediately turning a defensive move into an attacking one. To counter attack from a breakdown in play can be very effective, as the opposition are often out of position. **The basis of all defence is being able to tackle correctly and decisively**.

At the scrummage

This involves the back row often against an opposition back row attack. If the opposition are going right from their scrum the left-hand flanker takes the first player. The number eight takes the second player. Going left from their scrum the scrum-half will take the first player and the right-hand flanker will take the second player. The flankers must break and cover each side. To stop the opposition scrum-half making a break or to just put that player under pressure, one flanker and the scrum-half converge on him.

Another defensive measure, this time by the whole pack, is the wheel. The idea is to wheel the scrummage so that the scrum-half is isolated from the fly-half. This will limit the scrum-half's options.

From the line-out

As at the scrummage, always try and move in on the opposition scrum-half. Ideally this should be done by the thrower in on the blind side and either number five or six goes through the back of the line-out. If they have difficulty in getting through then the number seven can threaten the scrum-half.

At the short line-out, it is important to make sure there is a challenge when their jumper runs back. If the defence do not react quickly enough it gives the jumper a 'free' jump and an opportunity to set up attacks in midfield. It is less important to mark the jumper that runs forward. Near your own line the shortened line-out has several advantages because the non-participating forwards can stand just behind the try line and form a sort of double bank and quickly pick up any tapped ball.

The French forwards protect their scrum-half from the attack of the mighty New Zealand All Blacks.

Glossary

Apartheid The official policy of the South African government of keeping different races apart for jobs, housing, education and land.

Back row The flankers and number eight.

Backs The three-quarters.

Bad ball Getting possession of the ball so slowly that it allows the defence to get into position and break down the attack.

Blindside The area between the set piece and nearest touchline.

Box The area behind the scrum or line-out nearest the touchline and in front of the full-back.

Breaks Beating a player and creating a gap.

Corner flagging Defensive measure taken during an attack when one or more players make for the corner flag to which the attack is heading.

Covering A player who positions so that another player who is about to make a tackle is covered. This is a second line of defence.

Drawing a player To run towards opponents so that they are committed to an attempted tackle upon you.

Dummy To pretend to pass.

Dying with the ball To allow yourself to be tackled because it would be unwise to pass or kick.

Finding touch To kick the ball out of play over the touchline.

Fly kick To quickly kick the ball anywhere.

Forward rush Group of forwards dribbling.

Front row The two props and hooker.

Gain or loss line An imaginary line drawn through the centre of the scrum, ruck,

Garry Owen or Up and under A high kick in play to test the defence. The aim is for the ball and several of your team to arrive at the same spot at the same time.

Goal-line The line through the goals at each end of the field over which a try is scored.

Good ball Getting the ball, quickly from a set piece and without hindrance.

Grubber kick A punt which is aimed along the ground.

Half-backs The scrum-half and fly-half.

Handling Keeping the ball on the move by any type of pass or throw.

Heel From a set scrum the forwards will get the ball back to the scrum-half by means of their feet.

Infringement Breaking one of the laws of the game.

Interception Taking a pass intended for an opponent.

Loose forwards The flankers and number eight.

Maul A player holding the ball surrounded and held by players of both sides.

Pack The eight forwards of a team.

Quality possession Obtaining the ball cleanly and quickly without interference from the opposition.

Ruck Two or more forwards attempting to heel the ball backwards.

Set piece Scrummage or line-out.

Scrummage Where the two sets of forwards pack down after an infringement.

Shadow tackle To follow an opponent who has the ball; pretending but never actually tackling the player.

Torpedo kick A punt in which the ball revolves at a lower angle than normal.

Touchline The side boundaries of a rugby pitch.

Three-quarters The two centres and wings.

Useful addresses

Rugby Football Union
The Secretary, Rugby Football Union,
Twickenham, Middlesex, England
TW1 1DZ

Scottish Rugby Union
The Secretary, Murrayfield, Edinburgh,
Scotland.

Irish Rugby Football Union
The Secretary, 62 Lansdown Road,
Dublin 4, Eire.

Welsh Rugby Union
The Secretary, Cardiff Arms Park, P.O. Box
22, Cardiff, CR1 1JL.

Federation Francaise de Rugby
General Secretary, 7 Cite d'Antin 75009
Paris.

Australian Rugby Football Union
Executive Director, 353 Anzac Parade,
Kingsford, New South Wales 2023.

New Zealand Rugby Football Union
Secretary, Ground Floor, Huddart Parker
Building, P.O. Box 2172, Wellington 1,
New Zealand.

South African Rugby Board
Manager, P.O. Box 99, Newlands 7725,
Cape Town, South Africa.

Canadian Rugby Union
333 River Road, Ottawa, Ontario, Canada
K1L 8HP.

Books to read

Rothmans Rugby League Year Book by Steve Jones
(Queen Anne Press, 1988)
Rothmans Rugby Union Year Book by David Howes and
Ray French (Queen Anne Press, 1988)
Rugby the Records by Chris Rhys (Guinness, 1987)
Science of Rugby Football by Mike Davis and Donald
Ireland (Pelhams, 1985)

Index

figures in **bold** refer to illustrations